Alexander Roslin and the Comtesse d'Egmont Pignatelli

FIGURE 1
Alexander Roslin, Swedish, 1718–93, *The Comtesse d'Egmont Pignatelli in Spanish Costume*, 1763,
Oil on canvas, Minneapolis Institute of Arts

"a rather good portraitist for the times" Denis Diderot, 1763

Instructed in the art academies of several European capitals and, from his earliest professional debuts, boldly signing his pictures with the epithet *le Suédois*—the Swede—Alexander Roslin was, nevertheless, the consummate French court painter throughout the golden era of Enlightenment portraiture.[1] Between his arrival in France in 1752 and his death in Paris a mere five months after the execution of King Louis XVI in 1793, Roslin would reign as one of the principal portrayers of the French aristocracy. The nobility of Sweden, Russia, Austria, and Poland were equally enthusiastic in their pursuit of his redoubtable talents. His prodigious output, despite an exceptionally meticulous technique, made him one of the most renowned, and certainly one of the wealthiest, artists in Europe. He was, in a word, the perfect choice to portray one of the most captivating women of their era, Sophie Jeanne Septimanie du Plessis, Duchesse de Richelieu (1740–73; fig. 1), only daughter of Louis François Armand du Plessis, Duc de Richelieu (1696–1788), the genial companion of Louis XV and the primary rival of the Marquise de Pompadour (1721–64; fig. 2) for that monarch's favors.

In 1756 Septimanie married Casimir Pignatelli, Comte d'Egmont (1727–1801; fig. 17), himself the progeny of two ancient European houses, the Egmonts of Holland and the Pignatellis of Naples and Aragon. Louis XV witnessed their wedding contract. By 1763, when *The Comtesse d'Egmont Pignatelli in Spanish Costume* (a portrait now in the collection of the Minneapolis Institute of Arts[2]) was composed, both the artist and his sitter were approaching celebrity of a special order.

Septimanie de Richelieu, whose mother died within a year of her birth, received a traditional education in a Benedictine convent in Normandy, although her adult values were said to have been entirely fashioned on Voltaire's liberal polemics. Conversant in the arts, literature, and history, she could recite from memory the *Henriade*, Voltaire's epic poem celebrating the benevolent reign of the much-loved French King Henri IV (1553–1610). The countess's so-called "Spanish" costume, with its slashed, beribboned sleeves, surfeit of pearls, and raised lace "Medici" collar, was a type of fancy dress fashionable for its exoticism, but also for its allusion to the reign of Henri IV and his queen, Marie de Medici.

In England the style was known variously as "Van Dyck" or "Rubens's Wife" costume, and it was popularized in France at mid-century by two paintings of Spanish theme (fig. 3) executed in 1754 by Carle Van Loo for Madame Marie Thérèse Geoffrin (1699–1777),[3] whose legendary salon in Paris was the literary and artistic counterpoint to the Pompadour's more political and diplomatic gatherings at Versailles. The guitar with which Septimanie shares her *fauteuil* (armchair) in Roslin's portrait thus reinforces a Spanish sentiment—her husband was a Grandee of Spain and constantly entertained the Spanish diplomatic corps in Paris—moreover, she was an accomplished performer on that instrument (fig. 4). Her marriage at age fifteen to the older and more seasoned Comte d'Egmont was brokered by her father, and although it brought her tremendous wealth and social stature, was more a union of convenience than of bliss.

By the time she sat to Roslin, the countess was already universally acclaimed as one of the most perspicacious, glamorous, and *spirituelle* women of Parisian high society, and consequently both coveted and resented. The slightly junior Comtesse de Genlis (1746–1830) later recalled:

FIGURE 2

François Boucher, French, 1703–70, *Portrait of Madame de Pompadour*, 1756,
Oil on canvas, Bayerische Staatsgemäldesammlungen, Alte Pinakothek, Leihgabe der HypoVereinsbank

FIGURE 3
Carle Van Loo, French, 1705–65, *The Spanish Concert*, 1754,
Oil on canvas, The State Hermitage Museum, St. Petersburg

Madame la Comtesse d'Egmont the younger, daughter of Marshall Richelieu, at whose home I had dined several times with Madame de Montesson, was of a charming figure, in spite of her poor health; she was then about twenty-eight or twenty-nine, and had the prettiest face I have ever seen. She had far too many airs, but all of her expressions were pretty. Her spirit resembled her figure; it was mannered yet full of grace. I believe that Madame d'Egmont was simply singular and not affected; she was born thus. She had many great passions; she could have been reproached for a romantic temperament that she nurtured for a long time, but her morals were always pure …. Women did not like her. They envied the seductive charm of her figure; they wouldn't acknowledge her goodness, her sweetness.[4]

Unsubstantiated reports of liaisons circulated during and after her lifetime, including one with Louis Philippe Joseph, Duc de Chartres (1747–93), who would become more widely renowned as Philippe Égalité during the French Revolution. At a costume ball hosted in 1767 by the Marquise de Mirepoix, the prize for beauty was unanimously awarded to the countess, whose partner, the Duc de Chartres, "was the only man there worth looking at."[5]

While her noble birth and vast fortune made the countess an attractive *salonnière*, it was her intimate friendship with the cultivated bourgeois matron of the arts, Madame Geoffrin, that sustained her ascendancy within the elite society of artists and intellectuals known collectively as the *philosophes*. From about 1750, Madame Geoffrin regularly hosted two weekly mid-day dinners—a literary assembly on Wednesdays (fig. 5) and an entertainment for artists on Mondays. Every poet or painter of consequence clamored to attend these gatherings. The remainder of the week her salon was open to virtually any politician, diplomat, or foreign celebrity who chose to call. Like most Parisian salons, but perhaps even more so given the stature of her attendees, Madame Geoffrin's was an egalitarian forum for education and erudite discourse. Many of these soirées were followed by her *petits soupers* limited to a very exclusive party of her confidants. "I am so gay," she wrote in December 1766 to King Stanislaus II of Poland, "that a company of young ladies of [age] twenty come to see me when they want to be amused. Madame d'Egmont is at their head. She often begs me to give them little suppers."[6]

In another letter to Stanislaus, who had requested a portrait of the countess, Madame Geoffrin amplified her regard for her young protégé:

The figure of Madame d'Egmont is charming, but her greatest charm is when she speaks, which she does with a grace that cannot be portrayed, either in painting or sculpture. She has been painted several times, but no portrait renders her well. Lemoine, the famous sculptor, has begun her bust (fig. 22); if he succeeds, I must send you a plaster-cast of it; and I will tell Madame d'Egmont of the desire of your majesty, which will surely flatter her. [7]

Roslin's close friend, Jean François Marmontel (1723–99), author, playwright, and secretary to the Director of the King's Buildings, Abel François Poisson, Marquis de Marigny (1727–81; fig. 6), left a pertinent account of one of these *petits soupers*, where he often recited for the attentive ladies from his *Contes Moraux* (1761):

The feast was modest. It was usually a chicken, spinach, an omelet. The company was not numerous, at most five or six of her special friends, or three or four men and women of high rank carefully selected and delighted to be with each other…. [This night] a group was formed of three women and a single man. The three women, seated as if goddesses on Mount Ida, were the beautiful Comtesse de Brionne, the beautiful Marquise de Duras, and the pretty Comtesse d'Egmont. Their Paris was Prince Louis de Rohan. But I suspect that on this occasion he gave the apple to Minerva [Madame de Brionne], because, in my opinion, the Venus of this supper was the seductive and piquant d'Egmont. Daughter of Marshall Richelieu, she has vivacity, spirit, the graces of her father; she also possesses, or so it is said, his fickle and libertine temperament; but that is something that neither Madame Geoffrin nor I pretend to know. [8]

Marmontel further opined that the Marquise de Duras possessed a noble severity more appropriate to Juno and that the Comtesse de Brionne, despite her fine figure and traits, which one might consider an ideal of beauty, lacked the single characteristic required of a Venus; namely, the "voluptuous air" that gave Madame d'Egmont the advantage. Despite these often publicized rivalries, Mesdames d'Egmont and de Brionne were devoted comrades. The latter had been widowed at age twenty-seven in 1761, and at the time of Marmontel's reported supper with Madame Geoffrin, was the mistress of Etienne François, Duc de Choiseul (1719–85; fig. 19), the prime minister to the king. Both her portrait bust by Lemoyne and Roslin's portrait of her friend Septimanie appeared in the 1763 Salon—the exhibition of works by living artists staged every two years in the Louvre palace. [9]

FIGURE 4

Louis Carrogis, called Louis Carmontelle, French, 1717–1806, *Madame d'Egmont Playing a Guitar*, 1758,

Chalk on paper, Musée Condé, Chantilly

FIGURE 5

Anicet Charles Gabriel Lemonnier, French, 1743–1824, *Voltaire Reading his Tragedy* The Orphan of China *in the Salon of Madame Geoffrin, 1755*, 1812,
Oil on canvas, Musée des Beaux-Arts, Rouen. Dépot de l'Académie des Sciences, Belles Lettres et Art de Rouen.

The cessation in 1763 of the Seven Years' War between France and Great Britain brought a gush of British worthies to Paris. Horace Walpole (1717–97), the supreme gossipmonger of his era, arrived in September 1765, having recently published his popular gothic novel *The Castle of Otranto*. He would spend the better part of a year in the French capital, and, from his own effusive correspondence and journal entries, would appear to have been a regular dinner guest of the Egmonts and virtually a fixture at Madame Geoffrin's. Within two days of his arrival, he was confiding to Lady Hervey, "I have seen Madame de Monaco, and I think her very handsome, and extremely pleasing. The younger Madame d'Egmont, I hear, disputes the palm with her; and Madame de Brionne is not left without partisans." [10]

By December he was able to write to Lady Suffolk:

> There is a young Comtesse d'Egmont, daughter of Marshall Richelieu, so pretty and pleasing, that if I thought it would break any body's heart in England, I would be in love with her …. [She] is delightfully pretty, and civil, and gay, and conversable, though not a regular beauty like Madame de Monaco.[11]

In January 1766 Walpole penned a catty observation to the poet Thomas Grey:

> For the beauties, of which there are a few considerable, as for Mesdames de Brionne, de Monaco, and d'Egmont they have not yet lost their characters, nor got any.[12]

But to the Duchess of Grafton a week later:

> I figure you to myself in all your luster, and never lose sight of you, even when I am with Madame de Brionne, and Madame d'Egmont. The former has suffered from smallpox, but still has glorious eyes and infinite graces about her mouth. Her person is rather too tall and lean. The latter by no means answered to me at first, as her features are not at all regular. The more I see her, the more she pleases me: her countenance has endless variety, and one night that she came to supper where I was, in her nightcap with a cold and sore throat, made me have occasion for all my constancy. You see Madame how frank my confession is, though I am in neither respect so fortunate to be able to make it as full as the swain in the *Nouvelle Eloise*.[13]

FIGURE 6
Alexander Roslin, Swedish, 1718–93, *Portrait of the Marquis de Marigny*, 1761,
Oil on canvas, Châteaux de Versailles et de Trianon, Versailles, France

FIGURE 7

Allan Ramsay, Scottish, 1713–84, *Portrait of Jean-Jacques Rousseau*, 1766,
Oil on canvas, National Gallery of Scotland, Edinburgh

The reference in the last sentence to Jean-Jacques Rousseau's sensationally popular sentimental novel *Julie, ou La Nouvelle Héloïse* (1761)[14] was almost certainly sardonic, as Walpole despised his Swiss contemporary and actually, on January 11, had recited at a dinner hosted by the Egmonts the infamous and vicious missive he had forged under the guise of King Frederick of Prussia and sent to Rousseau, in which he offered the beleaguered author asylum in Potsdam, while satirizing his notorious paranoia with the proclamation, "I will cease to persecute you when you shall cease to place your Glory in being persecuted." Two days later Rousseau indeed fled certain government prosecution in Geneva and Paris for refuge in England under the aegis of the Scottish *philosophe*, David Hume (1711–76), who had served as secretary to the British ambassador in Paris from 1763 to 1765, but who was also, curiously, the antithesis in temperament of his impertinent Swiss peer. In March 1766, Hume commissioned Allen Ramsay's (1713–84) now iconic portrait of Rousseau in his legendary Armenian costume (fig. 7), but their relationship rapidly soured. Walpole's letter had circulated in French and British publications, creating a scandal that eventually precipitated Rousseau's divisive quarrel with Hume and his return to France in May 1767. The scandal also dampened Walpole's relationship with the countess, who was, and would continue to be, devoted to Rousseau.

While in England, the Swiss author composed most of his seminal *Confessions*, finishing them in Paris in 1770. Shortly thereafter the countess wrote to her confidant, Gustav III of Sweden, "I forgot to tell your majesty that I have spent five days in the country in order to hear Rousseau's *Confessions*. He only read us the second part: the first can not be read to ladies he told me." [15]

The French ministry, which astutely recognized Rousseau's prose as potentially incendiary, had permitted his return to Paris only under the condition that he not publish any of his writings. To protect him from prosecution and themselves from discredit, the Egmonts and a few select friends prudently retreated to their country estate at Braisne for Rousseau's recitation from his forthright autobiographical manuscript. When *Confessions* finally appeared in print in 1782, Rousseau had appended to his text a restrained but sincere compliment to his former patroness:

On reading my memoirs to M. and Madame la Comtesse d'Egmont, the
Prince Pignatelli, the Marquise de Mesme, and the Marquis de Juigné
…, [when] I concluded, everyone fell silent. Madame d'Egmont was the
only person who seemed affected: she trembled visibly, but she recovered
quickly and kept silent, as did the rest of the company. Such were the fruits
of my reading and declaration.

At the end of 1771, Rousseau, in an apparent gesture of gratitude for the countess's
patronage, sent her a collection of twenty-eight airs that he had composed
expressly for her:

Accept, Madame, the homage of an Old Muse whose desire to please you
can alone rejuvenate him. In these songs, although late in arriving, one
ought to discover some touching and tender melodies … they have been
dedicated to you: I wanted to make hymns. [16]

Walpole also returned to Paris in 1771, and although he makes no mention of
the countess in his diary, he does record on August 24 a visit to the exhibition
of paintings in the Louvre, which included a "Very good picture of the king of
Sweden and his two brothers by Roslin, a Swede (fig. 21). A fine portrait in crayons
by his wife."[17] It is the only mention of Roslin in Walpole's voluminous art criticism,
but then, he had little sympathy for non-British painters.

FIGURE 8
Alexander Roslin, Swedish, 1718–93, *Portrait of François Boucher*, 1760,
Oil on canvas, Châteaux de Versailles et de Trianon, Versailles, France

Roslin's immigration to France from Sweden was neither direct nor pre-meditated. Born in Malmö in 1718, he studied in Stockholm with the court painter Georg Schröder before establishing himself as a portrait painter in Gothenburg, Scania, and then Bayreuth. He traveled to Italy in 1747, studying and working in Florence, Rome, Naples, and Parma until 1752, when, with letters of introduction from Louis XV's daughter, Louise Elizabeth, Duchesse de Parme, Roslin darted off to Paris. Not until 1774 would he again visit his native land. The style of painting he brought to Paris has conspicuous parallels to that of the aforementioned Scottish philosopher-painter, Allen Ramsay, who had also studied in Rome and whose similar polished naturalism, innate elegance, penchant for neo-classical gravity, and extraordinary verisimilitude in the rendering of costumes may have a common origin in Italian portraiture, in particular that of Pompeo Batoni (1708–87; fig. 19).[18] As would Batoni in Rome, Roslin would be solicited by a bevy of foreign dignitaries and luminaries visiting the French capital.

Although the Swedish ambassador to the French court, Baron Carl Frederik Scheffer, quickly assumed the role of sponsor, the painter's meteoric rise within the xenophobic and staunchly Catholic French art community resulted more from the friendships with French painters that he had cultivated in Rome and from his early introduction to one of the most influential members of the French Royal Academy of Painting and Sculpture, Anne Claude Philippe de Tubières, Comte de Caylus (1692–1765), a distinguished antiquarian and raconteur. By all contemporary accounts, Roslin was also an adept if haughty courtier, and within a year of his arrival, he was admitted to the Academy, a crucial privilege that allowed him to exhibit his portraits in the biennial Salons. The Academy would elevate him to its council of senior members in 1767.

Another eminent academician who befriended Roslin almost immediately upon his arrival was François Boucher (1703–70). A much-lauded portrait of Boucher's wife figured prominently in Roslin's first Salon appearance in 1753, while her husband was the subject of one of the Swede's most engaging portraits of his *confrères*, which he exhibited at the 1761 Salon (fig. 8), together with his portrait of Madame de Pompadour's brother, the Marquis de Marigny (fig. 6). Undoubtedly, Boucher facilitated Roslin's introduction to the Pompadour circle, and several of Boucher's nineteenth-century biographers have further asserted that Roslin actually assisted in painting the drapery in the senior artist's regal portrait of Madame de Pompadour of 1756 (fig. 2). Roslin's virtuosity in the depiction of materials and fabrics was apparent in his earliest essays, and the proposition gains further

FIGURE 9 (FIGURE 2 DETAIL)
François Boucher, French, 1703–70, *Portrait of Madame de Pompadour*, 1756,
Oil on canvas, Bayerische Staatsgemäldesammlungen, Alte Pinakothek, Leihgabe der HypoVereinsbank

FIGURE 10

François Boucher, French, 1703–70, *Portrait of Madame de Pompadour*, 1758,
Oil on canvas, Victoria and Albert Museum, London

credibility if one considers the portrait of the Comtesse d'Egmont a transparent gesture of homage to both Boucher and the all-powerful Madame. It has also been suggested that Boucher's reduced portrait of the identically-posed Pompadour in a more chastened habit of a *campagnard*, or rustic, and positioned in a less rococo setting (fig. 10) was in part a response to unsympathetic criticism that greeted the more ornate portrait at the 1757 Salon.[19]

Roslin's submissions for the 1763 Salon included his portrait of the Comtesse d'Egmont, as well as those of Baron Ulrik Scheffer (1716–99), who had succeeded his brother as Swedish ambassador, and César Gabriel de Choiseul, Duc de Praslin (1712–85), French foreign minister and a favorite of Madame de Pompadour, who had just concluded the treaty ending the Seven Years' War. The Comte d'Egmont and the Duc de Richelieu had both distinguished themselves during the Battle of Minorca, which launched that conflict in 1756. The Duc de Praslin was also the cousin of the Duc de Choiseul (fig. 19). Another of Roslin's Salon entries was the portrait of Ange Laurant la Live de Jully (1725–70), a member of the Pompadour circle recognized as one of the more aggressive promoters of contemporary French art and, with the Marquis de Marigny and the Duc de Choiseul, a pioneer of the burgeoning taste for neo-classical furniture and design at mid-century. [20]

Baron Scheffer had cultivated a close friendship with Comte d'Egmont and his young spouse, and may well have persuaded her to sit to the Swedish artist for her first formal portrait, rather than to one of his senior French rivals, such as Jean Marc Nattier (1684–1766) or Jacques André Aved (1702–66). Whatever the source of the promotion, her portrait created a sensation when publicly exhibited. For the critic writing in the *L'Année Littéraire*, "… one could not surpass the truth and the beautiful execution of his fabrics; they are astonishing, especially in the portrait of Mme le Comtesse," although the same writer also queried the stark interior setting and the somewhat distracted visage of the sitter.[21] The distinguished polymath, Dennis Diderot (1713–84), who disliked Roslin's style from his very first encounter, nevertheless commenced his commentary on the 1763 exhibits with a clinical but tame description of the countess's portrait:

> He is a rather good portraitist for the times. I speak of Roslin … who
> has painted the Comtesse d'Egmont, daughter of Marshall Richelieu.
> The portrait is meticulous; her dress very close to satin. The flesh is a
> bit blanched, the brow a bit too much, the eyes are hard, but perhaps
> they resemble. The hand resting on the dress is well colored. In general,
> everything has an 'air blanc.' He aims for éclat and effect.[22]

The commentator for the *L'Avant-Coureur* was also struck by the unusual blanched palette:

> M. Roslin relies completely on frontal lighting, undoubtedly to demonstrate that he can paint without shadows to great effect …. He has produced, by means of all his white fabric, neither mass, nor repoussoir nor opposition, but this does not prevent his picture from being very brilliant, very gallant, very interesting, and the satin from being strikingly true. This tour de force is highly successful, but we caution anyone else from attempting such effects.[23]

If the daring deployment of an acre of iridescent fabric saturated in light from an imperceptible source threatens to flatten the figure's volume and heighten her flesh tones, it also serves to thrust her to the front plane of the picture and immediately imbed her physiognomy and features in the viewer's ocular experience and memory of the painting. This was definitely a risky if not reckless conceit artfully played.[24] Still, Diderot's unpublished ruminations on Roslin's portraits were exceedingly caustic:

> Roslin is Swedish. He is the most employed portraitist, but he is cold, graceless, and lifeless. He should be constrained to paint fabrics, dresses, lace, etc.—because he carefully nurses every detail—and to leave the face painting to others. Of all the portraits he exhibits this year, that of M. le duc de Praslin seems the best to me. One could scarcely find a more stiff and leaden portrait than that of M. le Baron Scheffer, Swedish ambassador; … I am no more pleased by the portrait of Madame the Comtesse d'Egmont, one of the most noble and seductive figures in Paris … for his having rendered, as so sullen, a person replete of so many attractions and charms.[25]

Two years earlier he had criticized the portrait of Marigny, asking if either the marquis or the artist had ever seen a portrait by Van Dyck, although he acknowledged that Roslin's portrait of Boucher was justly applauded for its beauty. The novelty and insight of Diderot's collective critical writings on art was his proto-romantic reverence for any effusion of genius unconstrained by conventions of subject and technique. Roslin, however, was an artist of his moment, which in French society portraiture meant more a sympathy for the staid, bourgeois tradition of the Lowlands than for ostentatious Flemish bravura.

FIGURE 11

Alexander Roslin, Swedish, 1718–93, *Madame Roslin, nèe Marie Suzanne Giroust, in Bolognese Costume*, 1768,
Oil on canvas, Nationalmuseum, Stockholm

The recent retrospective exhibition in Stockholm and Versailles,[26] assembling nearly one hundred fifty portraits, confirmed that Roslin was at the apex of his creative faculties during the 1760s, the crucial decade of transition in French art from rococo exuberance to neo-classical constraint. In addition to likenesses already cited, there exist the compelling group compositions *John Jennings, his Brother and Sister-in-Law* (1769; Stockholm) and the artist's *Self-Portrait with his wife, Marie-Suzanne Giroust* (1767; private collection), as well as engaging informal portraits, of which *Lady with a Fan (the Artist's Wife)* (fig. 11), the *Marchioness de Marigny en déshabillé* (1767; private collection), and the *Jean François Marmontel* (1767; Louvre) are exemplars of his skill at characterization. But of the formal, female portraits emerging from this phase of intense productivity and invention, that of the Comtesse d'Egmont remains Roslin's most brilliant conception and, notwithstanding Diderot's biased censure, a masterpiece within his entire oeuvre. Of necessity it almost had to be, given the stature of the sitter at court and among her patrician peers, and the invaluable exposure to those potential clients that her salon would afford the painter.

Common to the many surviving opinions concerning the singular beauty of the Comtesse d'Egmont is the estimation that it was primarily her animation rather than any physical traits that defined it. The utter absence in Roslin's portrait of any semblance of the "endless variety" of her countenance, which enchanted Walpole and Genlis, or the vitality and spirit observed by Marmontel, might credit Diderot's denigration of the artist's style as stiff and lifeless and the sitter's attitude, in this instance, as uncharacteristically pensive. However, a formal portrait is not for ephemeral amusement but for impartial posterity to contemplate, and a comparison of her likeness to those by other artists—Lemoyne for instance (fig. 22)—at the very least confirms that Roslin has accurately delineated her features. The objectivity of his representations here and elsewhere, which his virtuoso technique only amplified, thoroughly anticipates the sobriety typical of neo-classical portraiture. The question that begs answering is whether her "unanimated" demeanor was owing to Roslin's sensitivity to that emerging taste and to the specific dictates of his stylish patrons, or to some deficiency in his skill at capturing personality in paint.

The elaborately hand-carved frame (fig. 12) represents an exceptional example of a transitional French *le goût grec*, or neo-classical, style. The unidentified designer was possibly Honoré Guibert (1720–91), brother-in-law of Roslin's friend, the marine painter Joseph Vernet. Employed extensively by the court and by Marigny, who commissioned several frames in 1761, including one for his portrait by Roslin, Guibert may also have designed the neo-classical frames for Roslin's dual portraits of Boucher and his wife of the same year.[27] The classical elegance of the countess's frame complements the austere architectural setting and Roslin's deft treatment of nacreous satin and luminous flesh. The crowning emblematic *fronton* includes the laurel wreath and torch of Hymen and the bow and quiver of Cupid. Both allude to matrimonial bliss and confirm that the picture was commissioned by the sitter's husband.[28] However, it was likely his vivacious spouse who shaped the elaborate iconography of her portrait and thus the manner in which she wished Roslin to render her to the world.

FIGURE 12 (FIGURE 1 DETAIL)
Detail of the frame on Roslin's portrait of the Comtesse d'Egmont.

The individual components of the composition lend significance to the orchestrated whole and fashion a persona of exquisite refinement, intelligence, talent, and dynastic privilege. In addition to the several Spanish references previously discussed, the battle scene depicted on the wall to the left surely alludes to her husband's military exploits as a marshal of France. As recently as the year before, the count was elevated to lieutenant general of the king's armies. The mythological love scene in the spandrel above that picture depicts Jason and Medea, another Spanish allusion, in this instance to the chivalric Order of the Golden Fleece. Both branches of the count's ancestors were knights of that order almost from its inception in the fifteenth century. Casimir's election, undoubtedly

a foregone conclusion, would occur in 1767. The conspicuous trim on the yellow satin cushion is silver Spanish lace. The table, thoroughly in the new *à la grecque* style and capturing decorative elements of the frame, might have been part of the artist's inventory, as the same form appears in Roslin's portraits of Prince von Starhemberg (1762) and Count Peter Czernichew (1762), and very similar furniture figures in the portraits of Marigny (1762; fig. 6), Henri-Léonard Bertin (1768), Gustav III with his brothers (1771; fig. 21), and Gustav III in coronation robes (1777; fig. 15).[29] As previously observed, the arrangement of the countess's tranquil pose, her open book, scattered sheet music and attentive spaniel intentionally echo the devices of Boucher's earlier portrait of Madame de Pompadour. Roslin diverges dramatically from that precedent, however, in the greater severity of the countess's costume and setting, which is also imaginary but a nod perhaps either to the taste being promulgated by Marigny or to the setting of Van Loo's *Spanish Concert* (fig. 3). The appliqué flowers that cascade over Pompadour's dress are transformed into a delicious variegated still life that softens the cold marble wall behind Septimanie. The introduction of a landscape is extremely rare in Roslin's oeuvre and, in tandem with the opulent interior, could be intended to evoke the splendors of the countess's favorite country retreat, the Château de Braisne in Picardy, where Rousseau would recite his *Confessions*. Some notion of that place's import in her life emerges in a letter to Gustav III of July 13, 1771:

> I am here [Braisne] since Tuesday …. I feel great pleasure in once again finding myself in the woods. They are much embellished since the Baron Scheffer last visited, and it is a most agreeable place. The indoors are perfectly commodious. I have taken a very pretty apartment in which I have gathered together the occupations that make these moments of quietude so agreeable to me. My books … my guitar, my harpsichord. I ride horses, I fish, I hunt, I host small *fêtes champetres*. I establish little games by which the distribution of prizes brings pleasure to that portion of humanity which seems condemned only to labor. Finally, these simple pleasures keep me from regretting those left behind in the city … and this time of calm allows reflections that the tumult of Paris will not. I believe the little education I can claim I have had in the country, and I have spent several months here every year since my marriage and for the most part without anyone else my own age.[30]

FIGURE 13
Louis Carrogis, called Carmontelle, French, 1717–1806, *Madame d'Egmont in her Garden*, 1763
Chalk and watercolor on paper, Musée Condé, Chantilly

There is more than a hint of Rousseau's "natural [wo]man" in these declarations. His passionate prose descriptions of the effects of nature on feelings certainly resonated with the countess, as Rousseau himself observed, and if, in Roslin's portrait, she has not just left off reading *La Nouvelle Héloïse* to ponder its pathos and comprehension of the human heart, her attitude of meditative musing, which the spaniel fails to interrupt, might persuade a cultured acquaintance otherwise. Similar observations could apply to Carmontelle's watercolor study of the countess, also executed in 1763 (fig. 13). It is that quality of sentiment which her portrait conspicuously projects, and not any ineptitude of the painter. When she sat a few years later for her miniature portrait as a gift for Gustav III (fig. 24), she actually confessed to having posed as the maudlin heroine of a popular and lugubrious gothic tragedy *Euphèmie, or the Triumph of Religion* (1768).

A mere decade after the countess sat to Roslin she contracted tuberculosis and died without issue at age thirty-three.[31] The artist would survive her by two decades, during which time he would triumphantly return to Stockholm before passing several years at the courts of Catherine the Great in St. Petersburg and Stanislaus II in Warsaw. His final self-portrait of 1790 (fig. 14), painted in Paris as the French Revolution churned around him, reveals a man supremely at ease with his *ancien régime* affiliations, his wealth and stature, and his decorations, which included a knighthood in the Swedish Order of Vasa. He would outlive his assassinated royal patron Gustav III by one year and die peacefully in his private apartments in the Louvre on July 5, 1793, two weeks after the onset of the Terror.

Patrick Noon
Chair of Paintings and Modern Sculpture
Minneapolis Institute of Arts

FIGURE 14

Alexander Roslin, Swedish, 1718–93, *Self-Portrait with a Portrait of Gustav III*, 1790,
Oil on canvas, Malmö Konstmuseum, Sweden

NOTES

1. This essay is profoundly indebted to Joseph Baillio's exemplary monograph, *Alexander Roslin (1718–1793), The Portrait of Comtesse d'Egmont Pignatelli in Spanish Costume* (privately printed, 2004).

2. The painting was commissioned from the artist by Comte d'Egmont Pignatelli, by whom bequeathed to his nephew, Louis Joseph Charles Amable d'Albert, Duc de Luynes et de Chevreuse (1748–1807), Château de Dampierre; thence by descent to Jean d'Albert de Luynes Dunois, Duc de Luynes et de Chevreuse, by whom sold to Wildenstein & Co., New York, in 1998; purchased by the MIA from Wildenstein & Co., 2006.

3. See Baillio, *Alexander Roslin*, 14, and Aileen Ribeiro, *The Art of Dress: Fashion in England and France 1750–1820* (New Haven and London: Yale University Press, 1995), 162 ff. The two Van Loo paintings, *The Spanish Concert* and *The Spanish Reading*, were exhibited at the 1755 and 1761 Salons, respectively. In England the "Rubens's Wife" designation derived from Rubens's portrait of Helena Fourment, which at the time belonged to Sir Robert Walpole. Rubens's *Marie de Medici* cycle in the Louvre was another source of inspiration for French artists. See Ribeiro, *Dress in Eighteenth-Century Europe 1715–1789* (New Haven and London: Yale University Press, 2002), 275 ff.

4. Mme Carette, ed. *Mémoires de Madame le Comtesse de Genlis* (Paris: Michel, 1903), 51.

5. Wilmarth Lewis, et al., *The Yale Edition of Horace Walpole's Correspondence* (New Haven: Yale University Press, 1939), 3: 221, letter of January 22, 1767, from Madame du Deffand to Horace Walpole.

6. Janet Aldis, *Madame Geoffrin, Her Salon and Her Times* (London: Methuen, 1905), 293.

7. Comtesse d'Armaillé, *La Comtesse d'Egmont, Fille du Maréchal de Richelieu, d'après ses letters inédités à Gustave III* (Paris: Perrin, 1890), 126.

8. John Renwick, ed. *Marmontel Mémoires* (Clermont-Ferrand: G. de Bussac, 1972), 2: 169–70. Louise Julie Constance de Rohan-Montauban, Comtesse de Brionne (1734–1815).

9. The terra-cotta bust, now untraced, was a model for a marble portrait by Lemoyne, which figured in the 1765 Salon and which Madame de Brionne sent to Gustav III of Sweden in 1781.

10. Marie Catherine de Brignole, Princess of Monaco (1739–1813). See Lewis, et al., *Horace Walpole's Correspondence*, 31: 47.

11. Ibid. 79 ff.

12. Ibid. 14: 155–6.

13. Ibid.

14. On the reception of *Julie* in Paris when published in 1760, Rousseau later wrote in his *Confessions*:

> The opinion of men of letters differed from each other, but in those of every other class approbation was general, especially with the women, who became so intoxicated with the book and the author, that there was not one in high life with whom I might not have succeeded had I tried.

15. See D'Armaillé, *La Comtesse d'Egmont*, 180.

16. R. A. Leigh, ed. *Correspondence complète de Jean Jacques Rousseau* (Oxford: Institut Voltaire, 1981), vol. 18: 299.

17. See Lewis, et al., *Horace Walpole's Correspondence*, 7: 339.

18. Michael Levey, *Painting and Sculpture in France 1700–1789* (New Haven and London: Yale University Press, 1993), 190. Levey was the first to note the affinities between the Swede and his Scottish counterpart. See also Edgar Peters Bowron, *Pompeo Batoni, Prince of Painters in Eighteenth-Century Rome* (New Haven and London: Yale University Press, 2006), passim.

19. Humphrey Wine, *Madame de Pompadour et les arts* (Paris: Réunion des Musées Nationaux, 2002), 150.

20. Svend Eriksen, "Marigny and Le Goût Grec," *Burlington Magazine*, 104 (March 1962), 96–101.

21. P. Lespinasse, *Les Artistes Suédois en France au xviii siècle* (Paris, 1929), 18.

22. Jean Seznec and Jean Adhémer, *Diderot Salons* (Oxford: Clarendon Press, 1975), 1: 230.

23. Ibid. 176.

24. Roslin might also have been cognizant of Diderot's disdain for popular flowered silk dresses in paintings. He expressed this in his criticism of a Van Loo portrait in the 1759 Salon: "I don't like flowered fabrics in a picture. They lack simplicity and nobility.… However skillful the artist, he will never make a beautiful painting of a terrace nor a beautiful garment of a flowered dress." See Ribeiro, *The Art of Dress*, 59.

25. Ibid. 230–31.

26. Magnus Olausson, et al., *Alexander Roslin* (Stockholm: Nationalmuseum and Versailles: Musée National des Châteaux de Versailles et Trianon, 2007–8).

27. See Eriksen, "Marigny and *Le Goût Grec*," and *Early Neo-Classicism in France* (London: Faber and Faber, 1974), 189, pl. 66–7, 345–8.

28. As communicated by Joseph Baillio.

29. See Olausson, *Alexander Roslin*, 223 and 228.

30. See D'Armaillé, *La Comtesse d'Egmont*, 206.

31. The countess was apparently unable to bear children. This is implied in Voltaire's observation in a letter to the Duc de Richelieu of October 8, 1770: "Have the kindness to accept my compliments on the paternity of M. the Prince Pignatelli, since I can not offer them to you on the maternity of Madame the Comtesse d'Egmont. It is assuredly very sad that she does not produce beings resembling their grandfather and herself." Theodore Besterman, ed., *Voltaire Correspondence* (Paris: Gallimard), 10:435.

A French Countess
and a Swedish King

In February 1771, the twenty-four-year-old Crown Prince
Gustav of Sweden arrived in Paris. The event exemplified the
achievement of two goals: providing a significant component
of the young prince's cultural upbringing, and politically
shaping the future king's vision for his reign. The extended
visit was a confirmation of the long-standing and secure
friendship between Sweden and France. Gustav possessed
a keen affinity for all things French, and when he returned
to Sweden to be crowned King Gustav III (fig. 15), he had a
lofty aim: to create a "northern Versailles" in Stockholm that
replicated the celebrated the court of Louis XIV. He also had
a new friendship with a young countess, the beautiful and
charismatic Septimanie d'Egmont Pignatelli (1740–73), (fig. 1)
who would prove to be an enthusiastic correspondent over
the next two years. Until her untimely death, she dispatched
a prodigious number of letters to her Swedish friend, offering
advice, recounting details of her daily life, and often revealing
the political machinations and social intrigues of the French
court.[1]

Born in Montpellier, Septimanie was the daughter of Louis
François Armand du Plessis, Duc de Richelieu (1696–1788),
one of the most prominent figures in Louis XV's court. She

FIGURE 15
Alexander Roslin, Swedish, 1718–93, *Gustav III (1746–92), King of Sweden, in Coronation Robes*, 1771,
Oil on canvas, Swedish National Portrait Gallery, Stockholm

would grow to possess an entirely dissimilar character from that of her father, who, while proving himself to be a successful military strategist, maintained a notorious reputation as a careerist and roué. Septimanie's mother was Richelieu's second wife, Marie-Elisabeth Sophie de Lorraine-Harcourt (1711–40), who was descended from the celebrated House of Guise.[2] Three successive pregnancies had compromised Marie-Elisabeth's health, and she died in Paris at the Hôtel de Guise, her family home, on August 3, 1740, leaving the five-month-old Septimanie and a six-year-old son, Louis Antoine du Plessis, Duc de Fronsac (1736–91). Although Richelieu sincerely mourned his wife, after a short period he resumed his libertine tendencies by taking up with a young princess from the noble and infamous Rohan family. Septimanie would remain in Montpellier until age seven when, motherless and following the social practices of the period, she was placed by her father in the Benedictine convent of Notre-Dame du Trésor, a medieval abbey located in Normandy.[3] Incidentally, the convent's abbess was Marie-Gabrielle Elisabeth de Richelieu, the sister of Septimanie's father.

Cloisters such as Notre-Dame du Trésor traditionally tended to be managed by women from powerful families, and were utilized as a type of training ground, where young princesses and girls of nobility were sent for a proper spiritual upbringing. In these surroundings, the pursuit of leisurely pastimes would on occasion take precedence over religious study, and abbesses frequently entertained visiting aristocrats. Marie-Gabrielle was known to posses an engaging, kind, and energetic personality, and she quickly concerned herself with the education of her niece. Under her tutelage, Septimanie studied French, Latin, and history, learned to play the guitar and clavichord, and received lessons in painting and singing. These activities provided the girl with the skill set required for an "elegant and virtuous life," to which all French noblewomen of the *ancien régime* aspired.[4] Septimanie developed a particular fondness for French classical literature; in the heroes of Corneille, the tragedies of Racine, and the romantic idealism found in du Belloy's historical characters, she found fuel for her lifelong interest in politics, philosophy, social attitudes, and literary ideas, all of which would eventually be addressed in her correspondence with Gustav III.

In 1750, Septimanie found herself at the center of an important alliance between her father and his friend, the Duc de Belle-Isle. During a visit to the cloister, Belle-Isle and his wife suggested Septimanie marry their only son, Louis Marie, Comte de Gisors (1732–58), therefore strengthening the families' social and economic standings.

News of this proposal quickly reached the girl's other aunt, Anne Charlotte de Crussol, Duchesse d'Aiguillon (1700–72), and in order to halt the wedding plans, she immediately made arrangements for Mademoiselle de Richelieu to come to Paris. Thus began the second half of Septimanie's education, where she was mentored in the renowned salon of the Duchesse d'Aiguillon.[5] The duchesse had carefully cultivated a social circle that featured numerous luminaries of Enlightenment literature and philosophy: Montesquieu, Voltaire, Rousseau, and the *encyclopédistes*, among others. Although her soirées did not differ much from others at this time (with card games and gentle flirting being the essential ingredients), the duchesse, who possessed a great wit, refined manners, and a sense of impartiality, fostered the elegant art of conversation. During one of these gatherings, Septimanie was introduced to the acclaimed tragedienne, Mademoiselle Clairon, who agreed to instruct her in matters concerning elocution and deportment.[6]

FIGURE 16 (FIGURE 1 DETAIL)
Alexander Roslin,
The Comtesse d'Egmont Pignatelli in Spanish Costume, 1763

Another important figure in the girl's life during this time was Ulrik Scheffer (1716–99), a Swedish ambassador stationed in Paris between 1752 and 1755. Scheffer was a frequent guest at the Duchesse d'Aiguillon's elegantly appointed home, often visiting "even on weekdays."[7] He was quite charmed by the young Mlle de Richelieu, and encouraged her studies. In a serendipitous twist, his brother, Count Carl Frederic (1715–86), was appointed to oversee the education of the young crown prince Gustav of Sweden. Both of the Scheffer brothers had been deeply involved in the architecture of Swedish foreign politics since the 1730s. At one point, Carl Frederic had even represented his brother as the Swedish envoy in France, spending time in the Duchesse d'Aiguillon's salon, where he was introduced to her young charge. The Scheffers maintained close communication with each other; in their correspondence, Carl Frederic eagerly followed news of his brother's French friends, and often spoke of the young prince. In these tightly knit circles, Septimanie would likely have heard chatter regarding Gustav, only six years her junior.

FIGURE 17

Louis Carrogis, called Carmontelle, French, 1717–1806, *Comte d'Egmont Pignatelli*, 1758

Chalk on paper, Musée Condé, Chantilly

At fifteen years of age, Septimanie de Richelieu had beauty, charm, and as a corollary to these qualities, many suitors. Toward the end of January 1756, she was sent on a retreat to the cloister in Montmartre. One fateful morning, the abbey's superior, Madame de Montmorency, informed Septimanie that her marriage had been decided, and she was to accompany the girl immediately back to the d'Aiguillon home, where she could prepare herself for a meeting at her father's townhouse. Later that afternoon, a throng of family members gathered at the townhouse, and Septimanie was formally introduced to the Duc de Chevreuse and his brother-in-law, Casimir Pignatelli, Comte d'Egmont, who would become her husband. As one of the most highborn names in Europe, the twenty-nine-year-old Comte d'Egmont (1727–1801)[8] had already earned his place at the Versailles court. He was prominent in the military, achieving high rank in the king's royal army while serving in the War of the Austrian Succession, and highly educated, having completed his studies in Paris at the Collège Louis-le-Grand. He also possessed enormous wealth. A widower whose first marriage was by all accounts harmonious, the comte was a reserved man who "loved a good table and good books."[9] (fig. 17) While the match was a beneficial arrangement for Septimanie's father, it also seemed to be a good prospect for her security and happiness, and it came with a five-year-old stepdaughter, Alphonsine, to whom Septimanie would show great affection.

King Louis XV approved the union and on February 2, 1756, he signed the marriage contract, along with Queen Marie Leczinska and other members of the royal family, which was reported as a news item in the *Gazette de France*. Eight days later, a magnificent ceremony was held in the gardens of the Hôtel d'Antin, the Duc de Richelieu's lavishly appointed Parisian townhouse, and Mademoiselle Septimanie de Richelieu became the Comtesse d'Egmont, princesse de Pignatelli. [10] The couple resided at the d'Egmont home along the rue Louis le Grand, and kept a country home at Château de Braisne, near Picardy. Only a few days after the wedding, Septimanie's new husband, in his capacity as lieutenant general for the *armée du roi*, was called to duty in the ongoing Seven Years' War against England. Through an endless series of diversionary dinners and parties, Septimanie's mother-in-law began to introduce her into the highest court circles of Paris and Versailles.

The new countess was quickly accepted into this social scene, attending lavish lunches at Versailles, taking part in weekend excursions with the royal court to Marly, Fontainebleau, and Choisy, and even accepting invitations to intimate dinners in Madame de Pompadour's private apartments. But the Comtesse also found herself spending more time with a wholly different fashionable set: it is not a coincidence that she is featured in a depiction of the Prince of Conti's celebrated Salon des Quatre Glaces at his Parisian home (fig. 18). The prince and his mistress, the urbane and cultivated Madame de Boufflers, were known for their opinionated resistance to the royal autocracy, and were great supporters of the English constitutional government. With a remarkable tact and grace, the Comtesse d'Egmont moved easily between these two opposing social groups, which was a skill made even more impressive given the political and personal exploits of her notorious father.

From the Comtesse's and her friends' own letters, it is possible to reconstruct one week of activities in which she took part:[11] Sunday morning was spent at the Prince de Conti's home, followed by a late dinner for fourteen people at Mme du Deffands. On Monday, she accepted an invitation to dinner at the home of the Duc and Duchesse de Choiseul, and on Tuesday, she attended an evening dinner at the home of Comtesse de Valentinois. Wednesday, the Comtesse spent the day with a group of English diplomats at the home of the British ambassador, Lord Hertford. Thursday, she was present at a soirée at the home of the Duchesse de Praslin. Friday brought another dinner at the home of President Hénault. On Saturday, she dined at the home of President de Nicolay, with a select circle of couples that included the de Beauveaus, the de Noailles, the de Luxembourgs, the de Broglies and Mme de Boufflers. Interspersed throughout the week were visits to the homes of the Duchesse de la Vallière, Duchesse de Villeroy and Duc de Villars, and balls at the homes of the princesses of Monaco and the Palais Royal. Outings to the markets in Saint Ovide, Cousée and Vauxhall are noted as well, and her calendar was then completed with a visit to the races in Sablon.

This punishing itinerary was enough to drive anyone to exhaustion, and soon there was talk of the Comtesse's frail health, which began to hinder her participation in the incessant whirl of Parisian social life. Instead, she took to playing hostess for small, intimate gatherings in her own home with a select group of friends. Rather than the writers and *philosophes*, who were so highly sought by other salon hostesses, her guests comprised the elite members of French society, foreign diplomats, and artists. Frequent diplomatic guests included the Austrian minister de Mercy, the

FIGURE 18
Michel Barthélemy Ollivier, French, 1712–84, *The English Tea in the Salon des Quatre Graces*, 1766,
Oil on canvas, Châteaux de Versailles et de Trianon, Versailles, France

Danish and Swedish ambassadors Baron Gleichen and Gustaf Philip Creutz,
respectively, and the Spanish minister Don Joachim Pignatelli, Count de Fuentês.[12]
Favored artist friends included Jean-Baptiste Lemoyne, Chardin, Vernet, the opera
composers Grétry and Monsigny, and transplanted Swedish artists Per Adolf Hall
and Alexander Roslin. It was during this heady time when the Comtesse was at the
height of her celebrity that Roslin painted her portrait, arguably a high point for
both sitter and artist (fig. 1).

The Comtesse had several devoted female confidantes, including the comtesses de Brionne, de Grammont and de Mesmes, and closest of all, the Comtesse de Genlis.[13] During the latter decades of the 1760s, the women proved inseparable and were unwavering in their support of one another. This was most evident in a series of gossipy social scandals that surrounded the arrival of the disreputable new *maîtresse en titre*, Madame du Barry, at Louis XV's court. As various invitations to court dinners arrived for the purpose of celebrating the formal introduction of du Barry, the Comtesse d'Egmont and her friends would unanimously cancel them at the last minute. The comtesses d'Egmont and de Brionne were banned from court, and worse, demonstrated no public reaction, which enraged the king's new mistress.[12] Weeks later, the royal court planned an excursion to Louis XV's country home at Compiègne, and the countesses were provided the opportunity to right their wrongs. Again, Septimanie d'Egmont and the comtesses de Brionne and de Grammont sent eleventh-hour cancellations, setting off another scandal. The rivalry between the Comtesse d'Egmont and Madame du Barry continued unabated for years, flaring up again in the competition for the attention of the Swedish crown prince during his visit.

Amid the ongoing social intrigues in these circles was an undercurrent of political machination. The visible decay of the French monarchy fueled a deep mistrust in autocratic rule, and in the salons there was much discussion regarding the "philosophy of the throne." [15] Gustaf Philip Creutz, the Swedish ambassador to France since 1766, was a frequent guest at the salon of the Comtesse d'Egmont. Years before, while living in her aunt's home, the Comtesse often heard Creutz's predecessor, Ulrik Scheffer, speak of Gustav, the Swedish crown prince. Creutz, like much of French high society, was even more fascinated by Gustav, as the young man represented the hopes for a national renaissance—one that could possibly rival that of Louis XIV—in Sweden. For many, the Swedish prince embodied their notions of an ideal king, and they grew increasingly interested in enticing him to Paris.

This plan was, at higher political levels, already in the works. The French minister of war and foreign affairs, the Duc de Choiseul (fig. 19), had taken a lively interest in Gustav, and in February 1769, through Ambassador Creutz, the minister invited Gustav to meet the king. The visit would strengthen the existing relationship between Sweden and France; strategically, there was the hope that Sweden might serve as a French outpost against the great powers of Russia and Prussia.

As noted, Gustav was deeply intrigued by French culture and politics. He had great admiration for the *ancien régime*, and a passion for French literature, art, and philosophy, with a particular attachment to Voltaire. Later, as king, in a clever and ambitious stroke of one-upmanship, Gustav took the Polar Star as his personal emblem in a nod to the similar symbolic propaganda promoted by Louis XIV, "The Sun King." But of course the Polar Star never sets.

For Gustav, the French visit would allow him to seek assistance in strengthening royal power in Sweden, and it seemed that the royal invitation indicated the French king might lend support in the form of financial and political backing necessary for a shift of regime.[16]

It was determined that Gustav's brother, Karl, Duke of Södermanland, should depart first, and he arrived in Paris on August 24, 1770. On November 8, Gustav and another brother, Fredrik Adolf, Duke of Östergötland, set out for the continent, traveling incognito.[17] On November 16, they met up with Prince Karl in Kristianstad, who was on his return journey. There, Karl presumably provided his brothers with a full report of his Parisian activities. Gustav finally arrived in the French capital on the evening of February 4, 1771, where his first order of duty was to meet with Ambassador Creutz.

Creutz had some unfortunate updates for the crown prince. Over the past several months, events related to the Falkland Crisis between France, Spain, and England had unfolded to such a degree that the Duc de Choiseul had been forced from his seat of power, and sent to exile at his country estate in Chanteloup. The persons primarily responsible for orchestrating his ouster were Madame du Barry, Chancellor Maupeou, and the Duc d'Aiguillon. In addition, Gustav received the news that the old parliament had, "just a fortnight before his arrival" been sent into exile, and the hated Maupeou's parliament now stood.[18] Opposition ran rampant throughout the salons, where heated political discussions were the norm. Special outrage was reserved for the king's scandalous relationship with du Barry and his personal excesses. Meanwhile, the Duc de Choiseul received a steady stream of supportive visitors at Chanteloup, which only served to increase his popularity and profile. It was a critical time to arrive in Paris, and provided the ultimate test in diplomacy for the Swedish crown prince.

FIGURE 19

Pompeo Girolamo Batoni, Italian, 1708–87, *Pope Benedict XIV Presenting the Encyclical "Ex Omnibus"*
to the Comte de Stainville, later Duc de Choiseul-Praslin, 1757, oil on canvas, Minneapolis Institute of Arts

FIGURE 20 (FIGURE 14 DETAIL)
Alexander Roslin, *Self-Portrait*, 1790

The Comtesse d'Egmont, for her part, was profoundly affected by these recent political developments. It was her own father, the Duc de Richelieu, along with her cousin, the Duc d'Aiguillon, who had been the principal destabilizers of Choiseul's authority. The Duc and Duchesse de Choiseul were close friends of the d'Egmonts; his shocking removal from court, along with the long-standing members of Parliament, provoked the Comtesse into a lasting estrangement from her father and cousin. As a confidante of both Choiseul and Creutz, she was unsure how the crown prince of Sweden would now be received; of particular concern was whether the duc's successor would have the same interest in the Swedish court's ambitions.[19]

She had no need for worry. Gustav proved himself a flexible actor both at court and among the opposition circles. The day after his arrival, he called on the Comtesse d'Egmont at her home. The following day, he invited the Duc d'Aiguillon to dine at the Swedish Embassy. He also maintained his good standing with both factions by making his way out to Chanteloup to meet with the exiled Choiseul. Gustav's delicate diplomatic performance was fully tested on February 19, when he attended a dinner and a birthday ball in honor of the twelve-year-old dauphine, Marie Antoinette, at Versailles. While there, he also graciously accepted a dinner with Madame du Barry, where he presented her beloved dog Mirza with a diamond collar. Back in Paris, he presented himself in the sophisticated Parisian salons, where he brushed elbows with literary and artistic types, and spent more time with the Comtesse d'Egmont and her friends.

Through ambassador Creutz, Gustav and his brother Fredrik Adolf met with Alexander Roslin (1718–93), the Swedish artist from Malmö who was currently based in Paris. A few months earlier, the third royal brother, Karl, had sat for Roslin.[20] As Creutz notes in his memoirs, the crown prince and Fredrik Adolf passed several mornings in Roslin's studio, and the result was a series of half-length portraits of the three royal sons, works that would prove useful soon enough, and during the years to come in his role as Gustav's favored court painter. In his self-portrait of 1790, Roslin appears relaxed and self-assured, dressed in a sumptuously embroidered gold silk suit; it is revealing that he chooses to depict himself in the process of completing a portrait of his royal patron (fig. 20).

On March 1, the Comtesse d'Egmont invited Gustav to be a guest in her loge at the Paris Opera. There, he received the word that his father, King Adolf Fredrik, had died two weeks earlier, on February 12. He was to return to Stockholm for his coronation as King Gustav III, and he began making his arrangements to leave on March 24.[21] Before departing, however, he contacted Roslin and bestowed upon him a number of commissions for portraits of himself as the new king, as well as a group portrait of himself with his brothers.

This would prove both a boon and challenge for Roslin's career as a court painter. With the king already making his way back to Sweden, the pictures had to be produced from previous studies. Creating full-length portraits of Gustav III was merely an exercise in skillfully altering compositions and formats, but the group portrait presented a different set of problems, given he had only the three recent half-length portraits with which to work.[22] In the end, Roslin chose to depict the three brothers seated around a table, reviewing a campaign plan, and the result was exhibited at the Paris Salon later that spring (fig. 21).

While the artist was busying himself with these lucrative new commissions, the new king was making the long return journey to Stockholm, arriving on May 18, 1771. While in transit, the twenty-five-year-old king certainly had time to reflect upon his French visit. Even before arriving, he was writing letters to his new Parisian friends; aboard his warship in the Baltic harbor, he wrote to the Comtesse de la Marck of his adventure, "It is like a beautiful dream, but awakening is dreadful." [23] In the same letter, apparently for the purpose of exoneration against the accusation that he desired to be sovereign, he wrote:

I will show that I am careful [and possess a] good understanding, for common sense and humanity are established freedoms, and I loathe anarchy and uprisings. Within a short time, I will return to my native land. These laws, which during both of the last regimes have been mismanaged unsuccessfully, these I shall confirm by oath, and I shall be conscientious in upholding them.[24]

That summer and into autumn, as Gustav III settled into the business of being king, couriers regularly arrived with letters from France. Frequently included were missives from his new friend, Septimanie d'Egmont. While only her side of their ongoing correspondence is preserved today, it is possible to extract clues regarding the content of his replies; she often reiterated Gustav's questions or statements, and addressed them directly. She also wrote at considerable length, even playfully inquiring, "Would you be able to complain more about the length of my letter than you have done of their rarity?" (September 29, 1771) In these letters, she wrote freely of her feelings, thoughts, and concerns for both her homeland and her friend's new role.

She reminisced fondly of their time together in Paris:

> The other day I was speaking with [Ambassador] Creutz regarding some plans. I like him well—he is able to speak ceaselessly of you. We were in my loge, recalling the moment that fixed your destiny … we were speaking of your glorious future that at last has arrived! (May 4, 1771)

Her disgust with the French monarch was occasionally revealed, especially in the following observations:

> If we have a king that allows a mistress to choose him, I feel that there remains no one to serve our people … (March 25, 1771)

> [At] Versailles, I would have bought with my blood one tear of the king, but if you had seen his air of indifference, the boredom of the Dauphin, and the smile of Madame at this scene—yes, I am sure you would share the despair that I was feeling. (June 10, 1771)

FIGURE 21

Alexander Roslin, Swedish, 1718–93, *Portrait of Crown Prince Gustav of Sweden and his Brothers, Karl, Duke of Södermanland, and Fredrik Adolf, Duke of Östergötland*, 1771, Oil on canvas, Nationalmuseum, Stockholm

FIGURE 22
Jean Baptiste II Lemoyne, French, 1704–78, *Portrait Bust of the Comtesse d'Egmont Pignatelli*, c. 1767,
Terra-cotta, Nationalmuseum, Stockholm

In a series of letters dated June 27, September 1, and November 23, 1771, the Comtesse closed all three with a very real concern regarding her great rival, Madame du Barry: "One says that you have asked for the portrait of Madame du Barry, I was going to do the same [send you my portrait] until you write me and deny it all"; "it has given me alarm that you have asked for the portrait of Mme du Barry, but M. Creutz gave me his word to the contrary"; "I cannot send my portrait without a positive word that you never, ever have that of Madame du Barry—without a doubt, you would already have mine, but I cannot expose myself by being represented with her; this would be the height of ridicule. Give me your word of honor that you do not have it, nor ever will." [25]

In Gustav, the Comtesse found an excellent candidate on whom to impress her republican political ideals. The new king, however, proved tough to convince; his heroic principles were instilled at a young age, and he saw himself as the father of his subjects. This was a topic on which he and the Comtesse could not agree; she would occasionally chide him for his affection for an all-too-absolute power. In a lengthy letter written from Braisne, she found much to say on the subject:

> Honor means being submissive to your king without being a slave; try to be considerate but never forget that if you arrive by condemnable means, the biggest success [will mean nothing]—these sentiments are so natural to my soul—it is not that I do not understand ambition and that [I am an unsusceptible person] … it seems to me all men wish for power and ability and the means to attain it […] it is possible that your reign will become the epoch of our reestablishment of a free and independent government, but to be never the source of an absolute authority—a monarchy limited by laws appears to me to be the happiest of governments because I think that the aristocracy is so very removed from liberty and justice […] I think that you will do the goodwill of the Swedish people in extending your authority, but it will be regrettable if you do not create boundaries that are impossible for your successor to overcome, which will return your independent people to the stupidity of a king, some fantasies of a mistress and the ambition of a minister; your success will become the first principle of these abuses. Impartial judgment—she places the good legislator to the rank of the gods …. Your goodness and justice ought always to be directed by these principles, then the Swedes will say, "Ah, he has kept what he promised, and we are the happiest nation on earth." (Braisne, Sept. 1, 1771)

In June 1772, Louis XV named the Duc d'Aiguillon to the position of Minister of Foreign Affairs; the Comtesse still was not on speaking terms with her father, and the entire situation instilled in her deep feelings of suspicion and mistrust. Some months prior, she began numbering her letters and instated a system of delivery using double envelopes and numerous couriers. In August 1772, she closed a letter to Gustav with a series of complex instructions and a numbered cipher code to consult for his replies:

> It is still necessary that you have the tact to name no one from now on in your letters, [I have provided a number for you to use] for those who are personal … thus Mme de Brionne, Madame de Pignatelli, M. d'Egmont, my father and all the others [require a number]. With someone of interest, it is necessary to use initial letters, and two letters when the beginning of a name is able to be applied to someone else. For example, when you would wish to use the name of Madame de Bonfleurs—as "B" alone resembles Brionne, you should write "BO," […] I ask you again to begin numbering your own correspondence, and to provide me with a number code indicating M. Scheffers the eldest and the youngest, M. Fersen, and those who are of interest to Sweden, as I have done for France. (August 12, 1772)

One week later, on August 19, Gustav III successfully carried out an audacious and remarkable political revolution—a bloodless coup d'état—that in one swift moment completely overhauled the unstable parliamentary political system in Sweden, whereupon a new constitution based on the French model of absolute monarchy was established.[26] In an undated draft of a letter preserved among the d'Egmont correspondence, Gustav wrote:

> Here is the first moment Madame, where I am able to write to you since the big event that just happened here. […] I am able to make use of the state and I have been absolved during two days …. God who has seen my heart supports me, and I have found in my people an attachment and a courage without example …. Never has a revolution been able to pass more sweetly and more calmly than this one.

Her reply is enthusiastically supportive of his success. Sent from Brussels, where the Comtesse had stopped during a journey home from Spa, where she had spent two months taking the restorative waters, she wrote:

FIGURE 23
France, *Writing tablet case with décor commemorating the coup d'état of 19th August 1772*, 1772,
Ivory, gold, and enamel, Private collection

I would not exchange 10 years of my life for the morning of today [when your letter arrived] …. I have no doubt that you would never abuse this power which an elated people has entrusted to you without limits. […] In Sweden, one can say, as we say of our great heroes, "he was the conqueror and father of his subjects." At this time, I can only repeat, along with every one of your faithful subjects, that Stockholm is free and Gustav has won. [A childhood physician who has been accompanying me] arrived while I was weeping and crying out: "The King of Sweden is an absolute monarch!" He saw me shaking all over, without understanding what it meant. I covered my disheveled hair when the courier arrived. If it had been necessary, I would have repeated the same thing a million times …. I really need to know the news exactly as it happened. I ask you on my knees, to order M de Creutz to tell me the news. (October 2, 1772)

Upon the news of the revolution in the north, the Comtesse d'Egmont commissioned a writing-tablet case as a gift to the king. Commemorating the events of August 19, 1772, this charming object is inscribed with the words, "il assure votre bonheur," and inlaid with ivory, gold, and enamel (fig. 23). In a letter of October 14, 1772, she noted, "As soon as I return to Paris, I will have my portrait painted, because I hope to be completely well by then." Throughout her many letters, she occasionally mentioned the bouts of poor health that periodically confined her activity, and which even prompted the palliative visit to Spa with her husband and physician earlier that autumn. The Comtesse had contracted tuberculosis; it is recorded that she had submitted to an inoculation against smallpox years before, a procedure that in her time was quite risky, and quickly able to compromise a fragile immune system.[27] The portrait she refers to is a miniature by Per Adolf Hall (1739–93), another Swedish artist living in Paris (fig. 24). Seated in a gilded armchair, the Comtesse d'Egmont is shown dressed in an expensive costume of turquoise silk and draped with the famous d'Egmont pearls. She looks up from her letter—whose newly opened envelope lies discarded on the nearby table; the letter is probably one of Gustav's, the intended recipient of the portrait. Hall took a long time completing this small work, and Septimanie refers to the process in a letter of July 1, 1773:

> Your desired portrait has not arrived. I have thought about having an empty frame painted … it has been delayed because I have to admit that it had nothing in common with me …. It seems hard to encounter this woman on my own path to the painter's, who was born your subject …. Moreover, poor Hall has done all he could to make up for lost time, my health, and consequently, my face. They have been restored in a manner that makes my portrait look as good as possible. I assure you that I have spared neither time nor care to make sure it was made well.

In an undated note sent during the autumn of 1773, the Comtesse wrote to Gustav, "The sick woman is a convalescent for the third time. This beautiful season gives us more confidence that she can get better." She could not rally, however, and in the early evening hours of October 14, Septimanie de Richelieu, the Comtesse d'Egmont Pignatelli, succumbed to her illness. The Comtesse de Brionne and Alphonsine, Princesse de Pignatelli, the stepdaughter of the Comtesse d'Egmont, relayed the news in letters to the Swedish king. In a rather bittersweet turn, it was her husband who sent Gustav III the much-discussed portrait miniature by Hall. Generously, he also sent with it a terra-cotta bust by Jean-Baptiste Lemoyne of the Comtesse, which was exhibited in the Paris Salon of 1767 (fig. 22).[28]

FIGURE 24
Per Adolf Hall, Swedish, 1739–93, *Portrait of the Comtesse d'Egmont Pignatelli*, c. 1771–73,
Watercolor and gouache on ivory, Nationalmuseum, Stockholm

Three years later, one of Gustav III's courtiers made the following notation in his daybook: "Thursday, 29th August 1776—His Majesty had chosen white, green, and purple [as the colors to place upon a carousel lance, which indicated the lady he wanted to honor.] These were the colors of a French lady, la Comtesse d'Egmont, whom in France he developed strong feelings for, but now since she was dead, he selected her colors together with a cockade."[29] In one of her first letters to Gustav, Septimanie d'Egmont had enthusiastically remarked, "[the colors] green, lilac, and silver of your new order—they are my colors!" (Paris, November 23, 1771)

Erika Holmquist-Wall
Assistant Curator, Paintings and Modern Sculpture
Minneapolis Institute of Arts

NOTES

1. Twenty-nine letters from the Comtesse d'Egmont to Gustav III, along with two of his responses are preserved in the archives at the library of the University of Uppsala in Sweden (F418:143,149; F495:1–36). I am indebted to the efforts of Peggy Linrud and Jane Satkowski for their assistance in the translation of this material. For this essay, two publications proved invaluable: Beth Hennings, *Grevinnan d'Egmont och Gustav III* (Stockholm, 1921) and Comtesse d'Armaillé (née Marie-Célestine-Amélie de Ségur), *La Comtesse d'Egmont, fille du Maréchal de Richelieu, 1740–1773, d'après ses letters inédites à Gustav III* (Paris, 1890).

2. Hennings, 13. The powerful Guise ducal family, based in Lorraine, played a major role in the French Wars of Religion (1562–98) between the Catholics and Protestant Huguenots.

3. Joseph Baillio, *Alexander Roslin (1718–1793), The Portrait of Comtesse d'Egmont Pignatelli in Spanish Costume* (Private publication, 2004), 15.

4. Hennings, 26. The author notes that the young Mlle de Richelieu "was a dreamy child who fantasized, wandering in the cloister gardens and [becoming] a little nature-worshipper—a little Rousseauan, who in later life would befriend and admire the great philosopher." Mlle de Richelieu also became "quite religious at this time, and her practical aunt chalked this up to being a romantic, sensitive soul."

5. Hugh James Rose, *A New General Biographical Dictionary* (London 1853) notes the duchesse was "a lady of literary taste, who published a variety of lighter pieces and who is said to have retained to the last her good looks and vivacity, which earned her the name of *la bonne duchesse d'Aiguillon*, though the Marechale de Mirepoix said, "her smiles were as dangerous as the bite of the Duke of Ayen."

6. Baillio, 15.

7. Hennings, 59.

8. In addition to his French title, Casimir Pignatelli was the Marquis of Renty and Pignatelli, Duke of Bisaccia, Prince of Cleves, Duke of Gueldres and Agrigente, Count of Braisne, a Knight of the Golden Fleece, and a Grandee of Spain of the first class. Through his grandmother, Marie d'Egmont, he was descended from the house of Lamoral, to which the counts d'Egmont of Holland, princes of Ligne, and the former kings of Friesland belonged.

9. Baillio, 16. Three years after their marriage in 1750, d'Egmont's first wife, Blanche Alphonsine Octavie Marie Françoise de Saint-Séverin d'Aragon, died in childbirth.

10. Hugh Noel Williams, *The Fascinating Duc de Richelieu* (London 1910), 238. Officiating the ceremony was M. de Guenet, Bishop of Saint-Pons-de-Tommière, and the new Comtesse d'Egmont received as a wedding gift the historic Egmont pearls, valued at more than 1,200,000 livres. It is highly likely that these are the jewels featured so prominently in Alexander Roslin's portrait of the Comtesse.

11. Hennings, 104.

12. The well known Fuentês was not only at the center of a circle of notable Spaniards in Paris who spent a great deal of time at the Comtesse d'Egmont's home, but also a relation. In an interesting familial side-note, it was during this period in her life that the Comtesse decided children were not to be in her future, given the fragile state of her health. Her husband was rightfully disappointed, as he was the last of the French d'Egmont family tree. A solution to this matter arrived in the form of marrying Alphonsine, the Comte's daughter from his first marriage, to de Fuentês's son, Ludvig Gonzaga in 1768. To everyone's joy, a son was born two years later, thus securing the d'Egmont and Pignatelli bloodlines.

13. In her published memoirs, the Comtesse de Genlis relates a number of anecdotes about her friend that reveal the Comtesse d'Egmont's sense of humor. During the preparations for a play, the aunt of the Comtesse de Genlis had donned a dress festooned with apples and other fruits in order to play the role of Pomona. "The dress was heavy, my aunt was short, and her shape far from handsome …. Madame d'Egmont said she looked like a walking green-house." *Memoirs of the Countess de Genlis* (New York, 1825), 170.

14. Madame du Barry's published memoirs devote an entire chapter to the Comtesse under the salacious heading, *Intrigue of the Comtesse d'Egmont with a Shopman—his unhappy fate—the Comtesse du Barri protects him*. A tale of immorality (that was more in keeping with the character of the subject's father, as well as the writer, herself a ex-courtesan) is presented, which seems purposefully designed to humiliate and particularly cruel, given that the Comtesse had died some years earlier. In another anecdote, the Comtesses d'Egmont, Brionne, and Grammont are given their comeuppance, when du Barry generously forgives the Comtesse de Flavacourt for having associated with them in the past. *Memoirs of the Madame du Barri* (London, 1830).

15. Hennings, 143.

16. Magnus Olausson, et al., *Alexander Roslin* (Stockholm, 2007), 19.

17. Ibid. Traveling under the assumed names Count of Gottland and Count of Öland, Gustav and Fredrik's planned four-month itinerary allowed them to pay visits to smaller courts, and the pair made their way across northern Europe, stopping in Copenhagen, Hamburg, and Braunschweig.

18. "Gustavus III of Sweden and the Counter Revolution," in *Fraser's Magazine for Town and Country*, vol. LXXVIII, London, September 1868: 393.

19. Hennings, 164.

20. Olausson, *Alexander Roslin*, 100.

21. Hennings, 180. In the weeks prior to leaving Paris, the new king kept up his schedule of social engagements, visiting the Duc d'Aiguillon's country home, Ruel, where he dined with the Duc de Richelieu. On the evening of March 14, he hosted a private dinner for the Comtesse d'Egmont.

22. Olausson, *Roslin*, 100.

23. Hennings, 215.

24. Ibid.

25. Horace Marryat, *One Year in Sweden* (London, 1862) 396. The truth of this delicate situation can be found in this set of travel memoirs, published in 1862: "Gustav, like a man, swore he had never dreamt of such a thing. The confiding woman sent her portrait, and here after the lapse of near 100 years, the fair countess and du Barri hang side by side in the gallery of Gripsholm [the king's palace]."

26. While much has been written about this period in Sweden's history, thorough coverage of this event and its aftermath for the interested English-language reader can be found in the following: "Gustavus III of Sweden and the Counter Revolution," in *Fraser's Magazine for Town and Country* (London, vol. LXXVIII, September 1868: 391–410) and H. Arnold Barton, "Gustav III of Sweden and the Enlightenment" in *Eighteenth-Century Studies* (vol. 6, no. 1, Autumn 1972: 1–34).

27. Baillio, 17. See also Williams, *The Fascinating Duc de Richelieu*, 298–99.

28. Lemoyne also completed a version in marble, which was exhibited at the Salons of 1769 and 1771.

29. Gustaf Johan Ehrensvärd, *Dagboksanteckningar förda vid Gustaf IIIs hof*, ed. E.V. Montan, Stockholm, 1877, vol. I: 132.

EXHIBITION CHECKLIST

Pompeo Batoni
Italian, 1708–87
*Pope Benedict XIV Presenting the
Encyclical "Ex Omnibus" to the
Comte de Stainville, later Duc de
Choiseul-Praslin*, 1757
Oil on canvas
Minneapolis Institute of Arts
The William Hood Dunwoody Fund

François Boucher
French, 1703–70
Portrait of Madame de Pompadour,
1758
Oil on canvas
Victoria and Albert Museum, London

Per Adolf Hall
Swedish, 1739–93
*Portrait of the Comtesse d'Egmont
Pignatelli*, c. 1771–73
Watercolor and gouache on ivory
Nationalmuseum, Stockholm

Jean Baptiste II Lemoyne
French, 1704–78
*Portrait Bust of the Comtesse
d'Egmont Pignatelli*, c. 1767
Terra-cotta
Nationalmuseum, Stockholm

Allan Ramsay
Scottish, 1713–84
Portrait of Jean-Jacques Rousseau,
1766
Oil on canvas
National Gallery of Scotland, Edinburgh

Alexander Roslin
Swedish, 1718–93
Portrait of François Boucher, 1760
Oil on canvas
Châteaux de Versailles et de Trianon,
Versailles, France

Alexander Roslin
Swedish, 1718–93
*The Comtesse d'Egmont Pignatelli
in Spanish Costume*, 1763
Oil on canvas
Minneapolis Institute of Arts
The John R. Van Derlip Trust Fund

Alexander Roslin
Swedish, 1718–93
*Portrait of Crown Prince Gustav of
Sweden and his Brothers, Karl, Duke
of Södermanland, and Fredrik Adolf,
Duke of Östergötland*, 1771
Oil on canvas
Nationalmuseum, Stockholm

Alexander Roslin
Swedish, 1718–93
*Self-Portrait with a Portrait
of Gustav III*, 1790
Oil on canvas
Malmö Konstmuseum, Sweden

*Writing tablet case with décor
commemorating the coup d'état
of August 19, 1772*, given by
the Comtesse d'Egmont Pignatelli
to King Gustav III of Sweden
Ivory, gold, and enamel
Private collection, Helsinki